영어 리딩 학습의 최종 목표는 논픽션 독해력 향상에 있습니다.

학년이 올라갈수록 영어 시험 출제의 비중이 높아지는 논픽션. 우리는 논픽션 리딩을 통해 다양한 분야의 어휘와 지식을 습득하고 문제 해결 능력을 키울 수 있습니다. 또한 생활 속 실용문과 시험 상황의 복잡한 지문을 이해하고 분석하며, 나에게 필요한 정보를 추출하는 연습을 할 수 있습니다. 논픽션 독해력은 비판적 사고와 논리적 사고를 발전시키고, 영어로 표현된 아이디어를 깊이 있게 이해하고 효과적으로 소통하는 언어 능력을 갖출 수 있도록 도와줍니다.

미국교과서는 논픽션 리딩에 가장 적합한 학습 도구입니다.

미국교과서는 과학, 사회과학, 역사, 예술, 문학 등 다양한 주제의 폭넓은 지식과 이해를 제공하며, 사실을 그대로 받아들이는 능력뿐만 아니라 텍스트 너머의 맥락에 대한 비판적 사고와 분석 능력도 함께 배울 수 있도록 구성되어 있습니다. 미국 교과과정 주제의 리딩을 통해 학생들은 현실적인 주제를 탐구하고, 아카데믹한 어휘를 학습하면서 논리적 탐구의 방법을 함께 배울 수 있습니다. 미국교과서는 논픽션 독해력 향상을 위한 최고의 텍스트입니다.

탁월한 논픽션 독해력을 원한다면
미국교과서 READING 시리즈

1. 미국교과서의 핵심 주제들을 엄선하여 담은 지문을 읽으며 **독해력**이 향상되고 **배경지식**이 쌓입니다.

2. 가지고 있는 지식과 새로운 정보를 연결해 내 것으로 만드는 **통합사고력**을 기를 수 있습니다.

3. 꼼꼼히 읽고 완전히 소화할 수 있도록 하는 수준별 독해 훈련으로 **문제 해결력**이 향상됩니다.

4. 기초 문장 독해에서 추론까지, 학습자의 **수준별로 선택하여 학습할** 수 있도록 난이도를 설계하였습니다.

5. 스스로 계획하고 점검하며 실력을 쌓아가는 **자기주도력**이 형성됩니다.

Author Contents Tree

Contents Tree has published various English learning textbooks and teacher's guides. It also provides an English Reading Specialist Training Course for English teachers. At the same time, Contents Tree runs an English Reading Library named Reader's Mate.

미국교과서 READING LEVEL 1 ❷
American Textbook Reading *Second Edition*

Second Published on August 14, 2023
Second Printed on August 30, 2023

First Published on July 18, 2016

Written by Contents Tree
Editorial Manager Namhui Kim, Seulgi Han
Development Editor Mina Park
Proofreading Ryan P. Lagace, Benjamin Schultz
Design Kichun Jang, Hyeonsook Lee
Typesetting Yeon Design
Illustrations Eunhyung Ryu, Heeju Joe
Recording Studio YR Media
Photo Credit Photos.com, Shutterstcok.com

Published and distributed by Gilbutschool

56, Worldcup-ro 10-gil, Mapo-gu, Seoul, Korea, 121-842
Tel 02-332-0931
Fax 02-322-0586
Homepage www.gilbutschool.co.kr
Publisher Jongwon Lee

ISBN   979-11-6406-539-4 (64740)
         979-11-6406-535-6 (set)
(Gilbutschool code : 30537)

미국교과서 리딩 READING

LEVEL 1 ②

길벗스쿨

LEVEL 1 논픽션 리딩 준비

리딩의 기초가 되는 언어 실력을 키울 수 있는 학습 요소를 중점적으로 익힙니다.

영어 학습의 기초 능력을 다지는 시기로서 지문에 등장할 어휘를 미리 숙지하고 패턴 문형을 반복적으로 눈과 귀로 익혀, 리딩을 수월히 소화할 수 있도록 구성하였습니다.

미국 프리스쿨 과정의 일상 주제와 기초 논픽션 주제 어휘를 학습합니다.

● 권별 주제 구성

1권	2권	3권
1. Body Parts	13. Rain	25. Tree
2. My Brother	14. Spring	26. Housework
3. Family	15. Things in Pairs	27. Riding a Bike
4. My School	16. Animal Homes	28. Spider
5. Animals	17. Community	29. Hobbies
6. Seasons	18. My Room	30. Winter
7. Things in the Sky	19. Bad Dream	31. Vegetables
8. Shapes	20. Colors	32. Sea
9. Clothes	21. Food	33. My Town
10. Monsters	22. Transportation	34. School Tools
11. Jobs	23. Friends	35. Farm Animals
12. Museum	24. Sense of Touch	36. Five Senses

필수 패턴 문형이 반복되는 지문을 읽으며 문장 구조에 익숙해집니다.

글의 주제와 가벼운 의미 파악 수준의 기초 독해 연습으로 리딩의 기본기를 만듭니다.

· 자기주도 학습 계획표 ·

Unit	Study Check		Day
Unit 1	Get Ready	☐	/
	Now You Read	☐	/
	Check Up	☐	/
	Workbook	☐	/
Unit 2	Get Ready	☐	/
	Now You Read	☐	/
	Check Up	☐	/
	Workbook	☐	/
Unit 3	Get Ready	☐	/
	Now You Read	☐	/
	Check Up	☐	/
	Workbook	☐	/
Unit 4	Get Ready	☐	/
	Now You Read	☐	/
	Check Up	☐	/
	Workbook	☐	/
Unit 5	Get Ready	☐	/
	Now You Read	☐	/
	Check Up	☐	/
	Workbook	☐	/
Unit 6	Get Ready	☐	/
	Now You Read	☐	/
	Check Up	☐	/
	Workbook	☐	/

Unit	Study Check		Day
Unit 7	Get Ready	☐	/
	Now You Read	☐	/
	Check Up	☐	/
	Workbook	☐	/
Unit 8	Get Ready	☐	/
	Now You Read	☐	/
	Check Up	☐	/
	Workbook	☐	/
Unit 9	Get Ready	☐	/
	Now You Read	☐	/
	Check Up	☐	/
	Workbook	☐	/
Unit 10	Get Ready	☐	/
	Now You Read	☐	/
	Check Up	☐	/
	Workbook	☐	/
Unit 11	Get Ready	☐	/
	Now You Read	☐	/
	Check Up	☐	/
	Workbook	☐	/
Unit 12	Get Ready	☐	/
	Now You Read	☐	/
	Check Up	☐	/
	Workbook	☐	/

★ 이 책의 구성과 학습법 ★

Get Ready

기초 단어와 핵심 패턴 문형을 익히며 글의 소재를 알아보고,
문장 구조에 익숙해집니다.

QR코드를 스캔하여 정확한 발음 확인하기

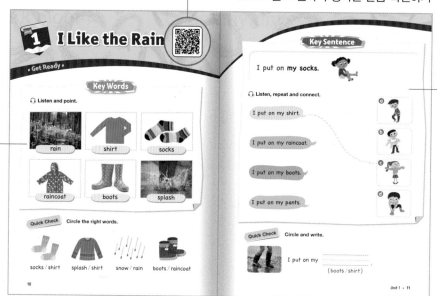

Key Words

주제별 단어를
듣고, 따라 말하며
익힙니다.

Key Sentence

글에서 접하게 될
패턴 문형을 미리
학습합니다.

Now You Read

일상생활, 학교생활 주제의 글을 읽으며 기초 독해력을 쌓고,
어휘와 문장에 익숙해집니다.

Reading Passage

그림을 통해 내용을
먼저 예측해 본 후,
음원을 듣고, 따라
읽으며 세부 내용을
파악합니다.

Pop Quiz

그림, 사진 관련
퀴즈를 풀며 글의
내용을 다시 한 번
떠올려 봅니다.

Check Up

다양한 유형의 문제를 풀며 읽은 내용을 확인하고,
단어와 문장을 점검합니다.

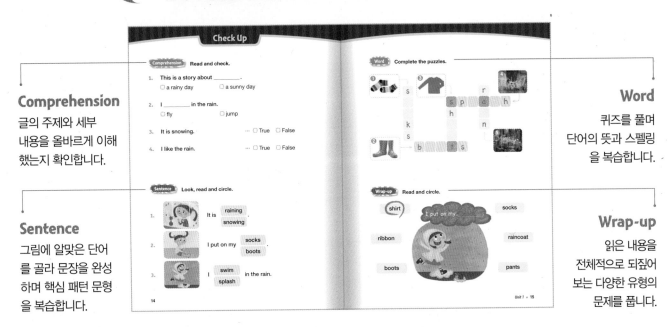

Comprehension
글의 주제와 세부
내용을 올바르게 이해
했는지 확인합니다.

Sentence
그림에 알맞은 단어
를 골라 문장을 완성
하며 핵심 패턴 문형
을 복습합니다.

Word
퀴즈를 풀며
단어의 뜻과 스펠링
을 복습합니다.

Wrap-up
읽은 내용을
전체적으로 되짚어
보는 다양한 유형의
문제를 풉니다.

Workbook

단어와 패턴 문형을
복습합니다.

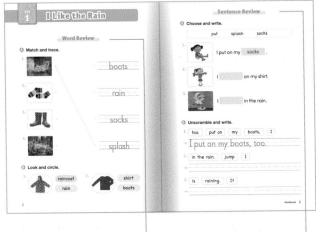

Word Review
단어의 의미를 확인하고
쓰면서 복습합니다.

Sentence Review
문장 완성하기, 순서 배열하기
활동으로 패턴 문형과 어순을
복습합니다.

무료 온라인 학습 자료

길벗스쿨 e클래스
(eclass.gilbut.co.kr)에
접속하시면 〈미국교과서
READING〉시리즈에 대한
상세 정보 및 부가 학습 자료를
무료로 이용하실 수 있습니다.

1. 음원 스트리밍 및 MP3 파일
2. 추가 학습용 워크시트 5종
   단어 카드, 단어 테스트, 문장 따라 쓰기,
   리딩 지문 테스트, 문장 테스트
3. 복습용 온라인 퀴즈

★ 목차 ★

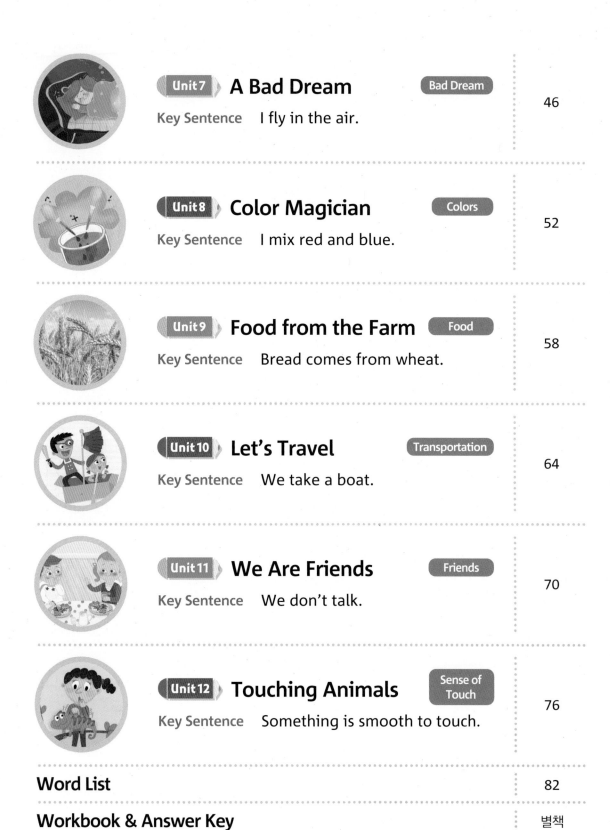

I Like the Rain

• Get Ready •

Key Words

🎧 **Listen and point.**

rain

shirt

socks

raincoat

boots

splash

Quick Check   Circle the right words.

socks / shirt

splash / shirt

snow / rain

boots / raincoat

I put on **my socks.**

🎧 **Listen, repeat and connect.**

I put on my shirt.

I put on my raincoat.

I put on my boots.

I put on my pants.

Quick Check   **Circle and write.**

I put on my _____ .

(boots / shirt)

I Like the Rain

It is raining.

It is boring.

Oh, I have an idea!

I put on my shirt.

I put on my socks.

12

I put on my raincoat.

I put on my boots, too.

I jump in the rain.

I splash in the rain.

Pop Quiz

What is the color of the girl's raincoat?

Yes, I like the rain!

Check Up

 **Comprehension** Read and check.

1. This is a story about _____ .
   ☐ a rainy day   ☐ a sunny day

2. I _____ in the rain.
   ☐ fly   ☐ jump

3. It is snowing.   ⋯ ☐ True   ☐ False

4. I like the rain.   ⋯ ☐ True   ☐ False

 **Sentence** Look, read and circle.

1.    It is   raining / snowing .

2.    I put on my   socks / boots .

3.    I   swim / splash   in the rain.

14

Complete the puzzles.

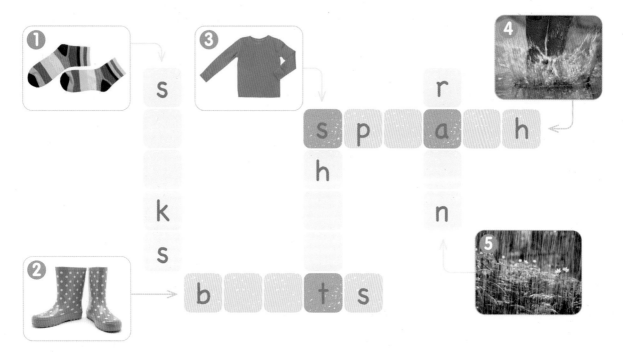

1. s
   s
   k
   s

2. b _ _ _ t s

3. s p _ a _ h

   r
   s
   h
   a
   n

Wrap-up **Read and circle the correct ones.**

(shirt)

socks

I put on my _____

ribbon

raincoat

boots

pants

Unit 2 Spring Is Here

Key Words

🎧 **Listen and point.**

snow

melt

flower

stream

bird

frog

Quick Check **Circle the right words.**

snow / flower

cat / frog

bird / dog

melt / stream

Key Sentence

The snow is melting.

🎧 **Listen, repeat and connect.**

The flowers are blooming.

The streams are running.

The birds are singing.

The frogs are jumping.

Quick Check   **Circle and write.**

The _____ are singing.

(frogs / birds)

Spring Is Here

Spring is here.
The snow **is** melt**ing**.

Spring is here.
The flowers **are** bloom**ing**.

Spring is here.
The streams **are** runn**ing**.

Spring is here.

The birds **are** sing**ing**.

Spring is here.

The frogs **are** jump**ing**.

Spring is here.

We **are** sing**ing**, too!

We **are** jump**ing**, too!

Pop Quiz

How many frogs can you see?

Comprehension Read and check.

1. This is a story about _____ .
   ☐ spring   ☐ winter

2. The snow is _____ .
   ☐ blooming   ☐ melting

3. Summer is here.   ⋯ ☐ True   ☐ False

4. We are singing, too.   ⋯ ☐ True   ☐ False

Sentence Look, read and circle.

1.  The birds are
   singing
   melting
   .

2.  The
   flowers
   frogs
   are blooming.

3.
   Winter
   Spring
   is here.

Word Find and circle.

flower

snow

s	f	a	b	c	h	k	p
n	r	q	g	f	a	k	e
o	o	r	u	i	p	n	l
w	g	s	t	r	e	a	m
q	h	m	c	d	e	g	y
f	l	o	w	e	r	s	e

frog

stream

Wrap-up Match and write.

1.

2.

3.

ⓐ The _____ are jumping.

ⓑ The _____ are singing.

ⓒ The _____ is melting.

They Go Together

Get Ready

Key Words

🎧 **Listen and point.**

pair

wear

together

shoes

mittens

chopsticks

Quick Check Circle the right words.

chopsticks / shoes

socks / mittens

shoes / shirt

together / wear

Key Sentence

Socks are a pair.

🎧 **Listen, repeat and connect.**

Shoes are a pair.

Chopsticks are a pair.

Mittens are a pair.

Gloves are a pair.

Quick Check   Circle and write.

_____ are a pair.

(Mittens / Shoes)

They Go Together

Can you find any pairs?

Socks **are a pair**.
We wear them together.

Shoes **are a pair**.
We wear them together.

Mittens **are a pair**.
We wear them together.

Oh, one more!

Chopsticks **are a pair**, too.

We use them together.

They always go together.

Pop Quiz

How's the weather outside?

 **Comprehension** **Read and check.**

1. This is a story about _____ .

   ☐ shoes   ☐ pairs

2. _____ are a pair.

   ☐ Shirts   ☐ Mittens

3. Desks are a pair.   ⋯ ☐ True   ☐ False

4. We wear shoes together.   ⋯ ☐ True   ☐ False

 **Sentence** **Look, read and circle.**

1.

   Chairs
   Socks   are a pair.

2.

   Chopsticks
   Spoons   are a pair.

3.

   We   eat
         wear   them together.

Complete the puzzle.

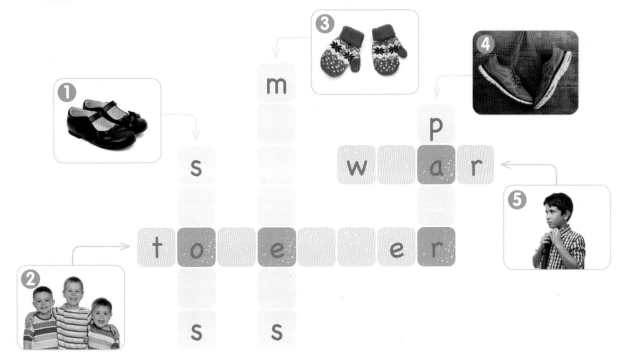

① s

② t o e ... e r

③ m

④ p / w a r

⑤

s ... s

Read and circle the correct ones.

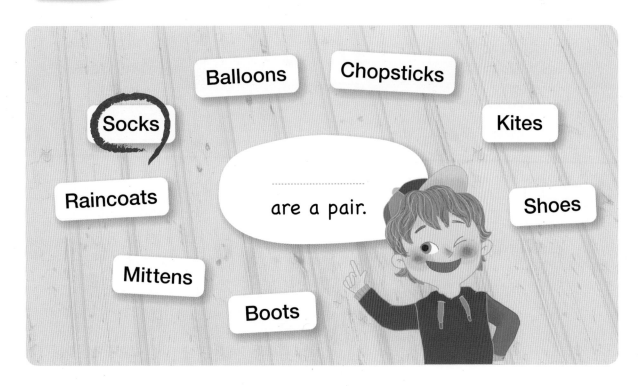

Balloons   Chopsticks

(Socks)   Kites

_____ are a pair.

Raincoats   Shoes

Mittens

Boots

Animal Homes

Key Words

🎧 **Listen and point.**

hive

home

nest

den

fox

web

Quick Check Circle the right words.

web / hive

nest / desk

den / web

home / bird

Key Sentence

A hive is home to a bee.

🎧 **Listen, repeat and connect.**

A nest is home to a bird.

A den is home to a fox.

A web is home to a spider.

A stream is home to a frog.

Quick Check   Circle and write.

A _____ is home to a spider.

(hive / web)

Animal Homes 🎧

A hive **is home to** a bee.

A bee lives in a hive.

A nest **is home to** a bird.

A bird lives in a nest.

A den **is home to** a fox.

A fox lives in a den.

A web **is home to** a spider.

A spider lives in a web.

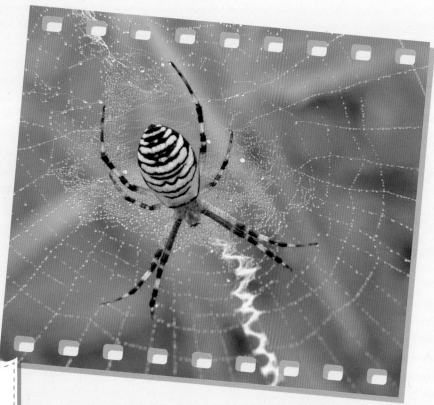

Check Up

 **Read and check.**

1. This is a story about _____ .

   ☐ animal homes   ☐ bees and birds

2. A bee lives in a _____ .

   ☐ web   ☐ hive

3. A fox lives in a den.   ⋯ ☐ True   ☐ False

4. A web is home to a bird.   ⋯ ☐ True   ☐ False

 **Look, read and circle.**

1.    A | den / nest | is home to a fox.

2.    A | web / hive | is home to a bee.

3.    A bird lives in a | nest / stream | .

32

Find and circle.

home

nest

n	e	s	t	o	n	q	w
a	m	d	v	m	e	y	t
d	p	e	h	i	v	e	b
e	x	c	o	m	n	e	t
n	v	m	m	q	a	b	e
c	d	f	e	e	y	t	b

hive

den

Wrap-up **Match and write.**

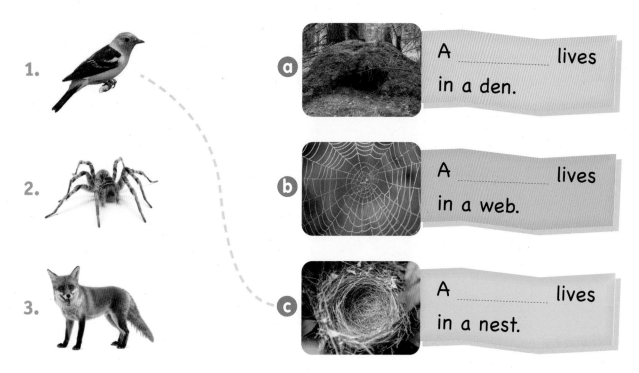

1.

2.

3.

a. A _____ lives in a den.

b. A _____ lives in a web.

c. A _____ lives in a nest.

The City and the Country

▪ Get Ready ▪

Key Words

🎧 **Listen and point.**

country

tree

hill

city

building

car

Quick Check Circle the right words.

country / city   country / city   hill / building   tree / car

There are hills.

🎧 **Listen, repeat and connect.**

There are many trees.

There are buildings.

There are many cars.

There are birds.

Quick Check   **Circle and write.**

There are _____ .

(trees / buildings)

The City and the Country 🎧

Farmer Bob lives in the country.

He likes the country.

There are hills.

There are many trees.

He can eat fresh fruits.

36

Peter lives in the city.

He likes the city.

There are buildings.

There are many cars.

He can move fast.

Pop Quiz

What is farmer
Bob eating?

Check Up

 **Read and check.**

1. This is a story about _____ .

   ☐ the school   ☐ the city and the country

2. Peter lives in the _____ .

   ☐ country   ☐ city

3. There are many hills in the city.   ··· ☐ True   ☐ False

4. Farmer Bob can eat fresh fruits.   ··· ☐ True   ☐ False

 **Look, read and circle.**

1.    There are many | cars |
                                            | trees | .

2.    There are | dens |
                                       | buildings | .

3.    He can move | fast |
                                         | slowly | .

Word Complete the puzzles.

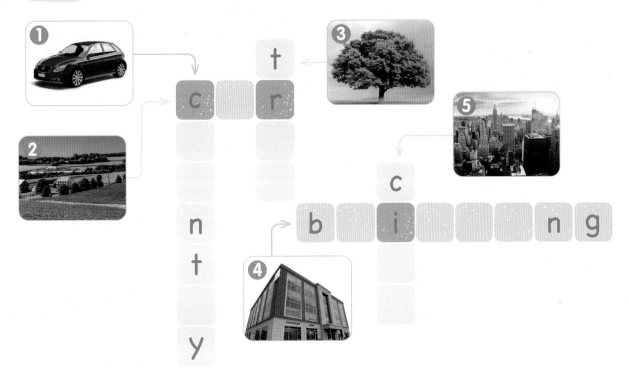

1
3 t
c □ r
5
n c
t → b □ i □ □ □ n g
4
y

Wrap-up Look and match.

1.

country

2.

city

hills

many cars

many trees

eat fresh fruits

buildings

move fast

My Messy Room

Get Ready

Key Words

🎧 **Listen and point.**

room

book

chair

pencil

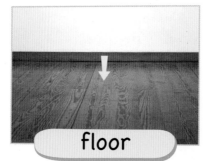
floor

messy

Quick Check | **Circle the right words.**

room / chair

floor / book

pencil / pants

desk / chair

Key Sentence

I like **pants on the bed.**

🎧 **Listen, repeat and connect.**

I like books **on** the chair.

I like shirts **on** the desk.

I like pencils **on** the floor.

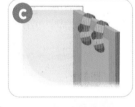

I like socks **on** the door.

Quick Check   Circle and write.

I like _____ on the desk.

(books / pencils)

My Messy Room 🎧

I like my room.

I like everything in my room.

I like pants **on** the bed.

I like books **on** the chair.

I like shirts **on** the desk.

I like pencils **on** the floor.

I like my messy room.

But my mom does not like it.

She wants it clean.

Pop Quiz

Where's the ball?

Check Up

 **Comprehension** **Read and check.**

1. **This is a story about _____ .**

   ☐ my mom ☐ my messy room

2. **I like everything in my _____ .**

   ☐ room ☐ desk

3. **My mom likes my messy room.** ⋯ ☐ True ☐ False

4. **I like pants on the bed.** ⋯ ☐ True ☐ False

 **Sentence** **Look, read and circle.**

1. I like shirts / pants on the desk.

2. I like pencils / books on the chair.

3. I like my messy / clean room.

Find and circle.

room

messy

a	e	i	e	o	h	v	m
c	s	j	r	l	u	b	e
h	r	o	o	k	c	v	s
a	s	h	o	r	p	m	s
i	n	p	m	q	d	g	y
r	f	f	l	o	o	r	c

③

chair

④

floor

Wrap-up **Look and write.**

1. I like books on the _____.

2. I like _____ on the bed.

3. I like pencils on the _____.

4. I like _____ on the desk.

A Bad Dream

Key Words

🎧 **Listen and point.**

cave

bear

jungle

lion

river

alligator

Quick Check   Circle the right words.

cave / river

alligator / bear

lion / bird

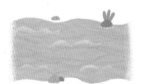

river / jungle

Key Sentence

I fly in **the air.**

🎧 **Listen, repeat and connect.**

I walk in a cave.

I run in the jungle.

I swim in a river.

I jump in the rain.

Quick Check   Circle and write.

I swim in a _____ .

(cave / river)

A Bad Dream 🎧

I fly in the air.

I meet a hungry eagle. "Help!"

I walk in a cave.

I meet a hungry bear. "Help!"

I run in the jungle.

I meet a hungry lion. "Help!"

I swim in a river.

I meet a hungry alligator. "Help!"

Help me! Help me!
Oh, it was just
a bad dream.

Check Up

 **Read and check.**

1. This is a story about _____.

   ☐ a bad dream   ☐ a hungry bear

2. In my dream, I meet a _____ eagle.

   ☐ happy   ☐ hungry

3. In my dream, I run in the jungle.   ⋯ ☐ True   ☐ False

4. In my dream, I meet a hungry frog.   ⋯ ☐ True   ☐ False

 **Look, read and circle.**

1. I walk in a
   | cave |
   | river |

2. I fly in the
   | air |
   | jungle |

3.  I meet a hungry
   | bear |
   | lion |

Complete the puzzles.

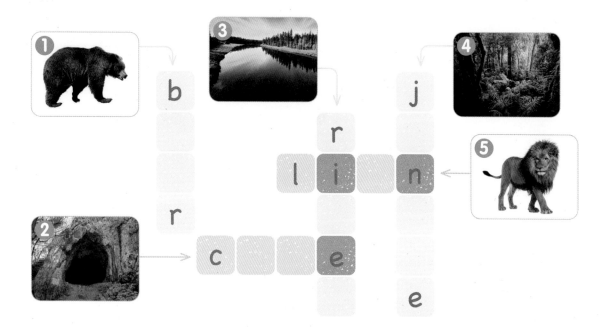

b

r

l i   n

r

c   e

e

j

Read and write the number.

In my dream,
1. I meet a hungry eagle.
2. I meet a hungry bear.
3. I meet a hungry lion.
4. I meet a hungry alligator.

Key Words

🎧 **Listen and point.**

mix

red

blue

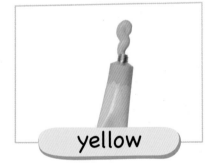

yellow

green

black

Quick Check **Circle the right words.**

yellow / blue

black / red

green / tree

mix / milk

I mix **red** and **blue**.

🎧 **Listen, repeat and connect.**

I mix yellow and blue.

I mix red and yellow.

I mix black and white.

I mix all the colors.

Quick Check **Circle and write.**

I mix _____ and yellow.

(green / red)

Color Magician 🎧

I am a color magician.

I make colors.

I mix red **and** blue.

That makes purple.

I mix yellow **and** blue.

That makes green.

I mix red **and** yellow.

That makes orange.

I mix black **and** white.

That makes gray.

I mix all the colors.

Oh, I made a monster!

Pop Quiz

What is the color of the monster?

 **Read and check.**

1. This is a story about _____ .

   ☐ colors   ☐ shapes

2. I _____ colors.

   ☐ make   ☐ draw

3. I am a book magician.   ⋯ ☐ True   ☐ False

4. I made a monster.   ⋯ ☐ True   ☐ False

 **Look, read and circle.**

1.  I mix yellow and black / blue .

2.  I mix black and gray / white .

3.  That makes orange / green .

Find and circle.

①

blue

②

black

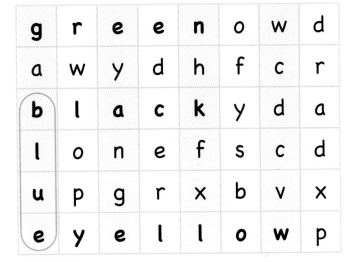

g	r	e	e	n	o	w	d
a	w	y	d	h	f	c	r
b	l	a	c	k	y	d	a
l	o	n	e	f	s	c	d
u	p	g	r	x	b	v	x
e	y	e	l	l	o	w	p

③

green

④

yellow

Wrap-up **Look and write.**

1. I mix yellow and blue.
   That makes _____.

2. I mix black and _____.
   That makes gray.

3. I mix red and _____.
   That makes purple.

4. I mix red and yellow.
   That makes _____.

Food from the Farm

Key Words

🎧 **Listen and point.**

bread

wheat

tomato

grow

farm

milk

Quick Check   Circle the right words.

bread / tomato   egg / wheat   corn / milk   farm / flower

Bread comes from wheat.

🎧 **Listen, repeat and connect.**

Ketchup **comes from** tomatoes.

Eggs **come from** hens.

Milk **comes from** cows.

Cheese **comes from** cows.

Quick Check Circle and write.

_____ come from hens.

(Eggs / Milk)

Food from the Farm 🎧

It is lunch time!
Where does food come
from?

Bread **comes from**
wheat.

Ketchup **comes from**
tomatoes.

Wheat and tomatoes grow on the farm.

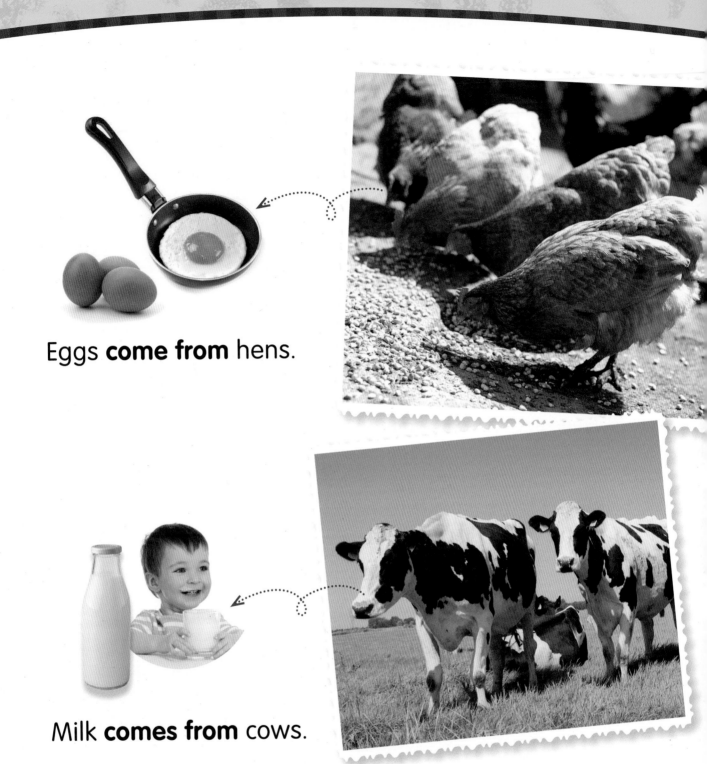

Eggs **come from** hens.

Milk **comes from** cows.

Hens and cows live on the farm.

What else comes from a farm?

Pop Quiz

What animals can you see?

 **Comprehension**   **Read and check.**

1. **This is a story about _____ .**

   ☐ foods for animal   ☐ foods from a farm

2. **Wheat and tomatoes grow on the _____ .**

   ☐ farm   ☐ city

3. **Milk comes from hens.**   ··· ☐ True   ☐ False

4. **Hens and cows live on the farm.**   ··· ☐ True   ☐ False

 **Sentence**   **Look, read and circle.**

1.  | Ketchup | comes from tomatoes.
   | Cheese |

2. | Milk | comes from wheat.
   | Bread |

3.   Wheat and tomatoes | grow | on the farm.
   | come |

Word Complete the puzzles.

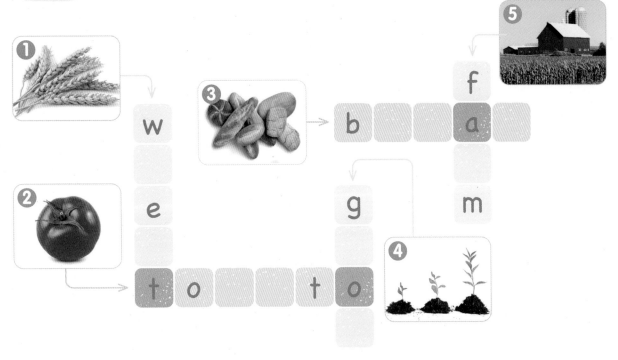

	w						f	
			b				a	
	e					g	m	
t	o				t	o		

Wrap-up Match and write.

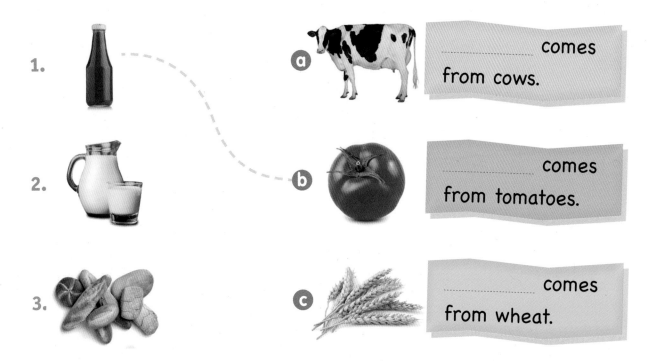

1.

a _____ comes from cows.

2.

b _____ comes from tomatoes.

3.

c _____ comes from wheat.

Let's Travel

Key Words

🎧 **Listen and point.**

boat

sail

drive

road

train

railroad

Quick Check **Circle the right words.**

train / tree

sail / road

drive / railroad

bus / boat

Key Sentence

We take **a boat.**

🎧 **Listen, repeat and connect.**

We take a bus.

We take a plane.

We take a train.

We take a car.

Quick Check **Circle and write.**

We take a _____ .

(bus / boat)

Let's Travel 🎧

We take a boat. Row! Row!

Let's sail across the river.

We take a bus. Vroom! Vroom!

Let's drive on the road.

We take a plane. Zoom! Zoom!

Let's fly in the air.

We take a train. Choo! Choo!

Let's run on the railroad.

Pop Quiz

What is the girl with a blue hat doing?

Check Up

 **Read and check.**

1. This is a story about _____ .

☐ travel ☐ weather

2. Let's sail across the _____ .

☐ air ☐ river

3. We take a plane. ⋯ ☐ True ☐ False

4. Let's fly on the road. ⋯ ☐ True ☐ False

 **Look, read and circle.**

1.  We take a
train
boat
.

2.  We take a
plane
bus
.

3.  Let's run on the
river
railroad
.

Find and circle.

1

train

2

road

t	o	g	o	b	t	f	s
r	p	r	t	i	d	v	a
a	q	s	r	c	m	x	i
i	s	g	o	r	l	m	l
n	x	d	a	w	h	f	m
a	b	c	d	r	i	v	e

3

drive

4

sail

Wrap-up **Look and write.**

1. We take a _____ .
   Let's fly in the _____ .

2. We take a _____ .
   Let's drive on the _____ .

3. We take a _____ .
   Let's sail across the _____ .

4. We take a _____ .
   Let's run on the _____ .

Unit 11 We Are Friends

■ Get Ready ■

Key Words

🎧 **Listen and point.**

fight

talk

share

smile

toys

friends

Quick Check   Circle the right words.

talk / fight

share / smile

toys / trees

frogs / friends

We don't talk.

🎧 **Listen, repeat and connect.**

We share toys.

We eat lunch together.

We don't share books.

We don't eat together.

Quick Check   Circle and write.

We share _____ .

(books / toys)

We Are Friends

Sometimes, **we fight**.

Then, **we don't talk**.

We don't share books.

We don't eat together.

But soon, she smiles at me.

I smile back.

72

Then, **we talk** together.

We share toys.

We eat lunch together.

Do you know who we are?

That's right. We are friends!

Check Up

 **Read and check.**

1. This is a story about _____ .

   ☐ toys ☐ friends

2. Sometimes, we _____ .

   ☐ fight ☐ fly

3. We are friends. ⋯ ☐ True ☐ False

4. We don't fight. ⋯ ☐ True ☐ False

 **Look, read and circle.**

1.  We don't fight / eat together.

2.  We share / talk toys.

3.  She fights / smiles at me.

74

s h _ _ e

f i _ _ t

t _ _ k

e

y

s

Wrap-up Look and write.

1. We **talk** together. ⟷ We _____ together.

2. We _____ toys. ⟷ We **don't share** toys.

3. We **eat** lunch together. ⟷ We _____ lunch together.

Unit 12 Touching Animals

Key Words

🎧 **Listen and point.**

touch

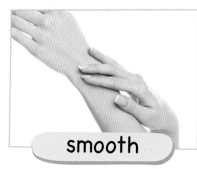
smooth

cool

rough

soft

spiky

Quick Check Circle the right words.

smooth / spiky

sail / soft

rough / smooth

hot / cool

Something is **smooth** to touch.

🎧 **Listen, repeat and connect.**

Something is cool to touch.

 **a**

Something is rough to touch.

 **b**

Something is soft to touch.

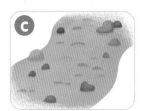 **c**

Something is spiky to touch.

 **d**

Quick Check **Circle and write.**

Something is _____ to touch.

(spiky / soft)

Touching Animals

There are many animals in the jungle.

Something is smooth **to touch.**

Oh, it's a snake!

Something is cool **to touch.**

Oh, it's an iguana!

Something is rough **to touch**.
Oh, it's a turtle!

Something is soft **to touch**.
Oh, it's a monkey!

Something is spiky **to touch**.
Oh, it's a hedgehog!

Pop Quiz

What animals are the kids touching?

Comprehension Read and check.

1. This is a story about _____ animals.
    ☐ drawing   ☐ touching

2. A snake is _____ to touch.
    ☐ smooth   ☐ hot

3. A turtle is spiky to touch.   ⋯ ☐ True   ☐ False

4. There are many animals in the jungle.   ⋯ ☐ True   ☐ False

Sentence Look, read and circle.

1.  Something is spiky / smooth to touch.

2.  Something is rough / soft to touch.

3.  It's a monkey / hedgehog !

Find and circle.

①
smooth

②
touch

s	o	b	t	p	o	i	f
m	s	c	o	o	l	c	r
o	w	o	u	c	s	f	o
o	p	l	c	m	x	c	u
t	a	c	h	b	d	f	g
h	e	u	t	a	v	x	h

③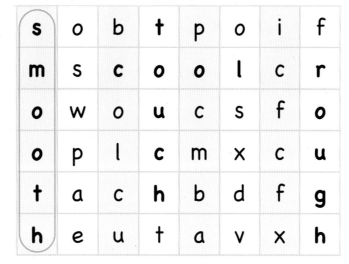
rough

④
cool

Wrap-up **Look and match.**

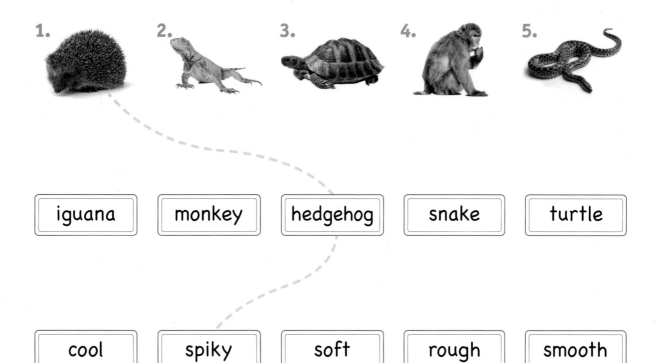

1. 2. 3. 4. 5.

| iguana | monkey | hedgehog | snake | turtle |

| cool | spiky | soft | rough | smooth |

WORD LIST

· Unit 1 ·	· Unit 2 ·	· Unit 3 ·
I Like the Rain	**Spring Is Here**	**They Go Together**

Unit 1		Unit 2		Unit 3	
☐ boots	장화	☐ bird	새	☐ always	항상, 언제나
☐ boring	지루한, 재미없는	☐ bloom	꽃이 피다	☐ chopsticks	젓가락
☐ have	가지고 있다	☐ flower	꽃	☐ find	찾다, 발견하다
☐ idea	아이디어, 생각	☐ frog	개구리	☐ gloves	장갑
☐ like	좋아하다	☐ be here	여기에 있다, 오다	☐ go	가다
☐ pants	바지	☐ jump	뛰다, 점프하다	☐ mittens	손모아장갑
☐ put on	～을 입다, 신다	☐ melt	녹다	☐ pair	한 쌍
☐ rain	비; 비가 오다	☐ run	흐르다, 달리다	☐ shoes	신발
☐ raincoat	비옷	☐ sing	노래하다	☐ together	함께
☐ shirt	셔츠, 티셔츠	☐ snow	눈; 눈이 오다	☐ wear	입다, 신다
☐ socks	양말	☐ spring	봄		
☐ splash	첨벙거리다	☐ stream	시냇물		

· Unit 4 ·
Animal Homes

- [ ] bee — 벌
- [ ] den — (야생 동물이 사는) 굴
- [ ] fox — 여우
- [ ] hive — 벌집
- [ ] home — 집
- [ ] live — 살다
- [ ] nest — 둥지
- [ ] spider — 거미
- [ ] web — 거미줄

· Unit 5 ·
The City and the Country

- [ ] building — 빌딩
- [ ] car — 자동차
- [ ] city — 도시
- [ ] country — 시골
- [ ] farmer — 농부
- [ ] fast — 빨리, 빠른
- [ ] fresh — 신선한, 갓 딴
- [ ] fruit — 과일
- [ ] hill — 언덕
- [ ] like — 좋아하다
- [ ] many — 많은
- [ ] move — 이동하다, 움직이다
- [ ] tree — 나무

· Unit 6 ·
My Messy Room

- [ ] book — 책
- [ ] chair — 의자
- [ ] clean — 깨끗한; 청소하다
- [ ] desk — 책상
- [ ] door — 문
- [ ] everything — 모든 것
- [ ] floor — 바닥
- [ ] in — ~ 안에
- [ ] messy — 지저분한, 엉망인
- [ ] mom — 엄마
- [ ] on — ~ 위에
- [ ] pencil — 연필
- [ ] room — 방
- [ ] want — 원하다

· Unit 7 ·
A Bad Dream

- [ ] air — 하늘
- [ ] alligator — 악어
- [ ] bad dream — 악몽
- [ ] bear — 곰
- [ ] cave — 동굴
- [ ] eagle — 독수리
- [ ] fly — 날다
- [ ] help — 돕다

- [ ] hungry — 배고픈, 굶주린
- [ ] jungle — 정글
- [ ] lion — 사자
- [ ] meet — 만나다
- [ ] river — 강
- [ ] run — 달리다
- [ ] swim — 수영하다
- [ ] walk — 걷다

· Unit 8 ·
Color Magician

- [ ] black — 검은색
- [ ] blue — 파란색
- [ ] color — 색, 색깔
- [ ] gray — 회색
- [ ] green — 초록색
- [ ] magician — 마술사, 마법사
- [ ] mix — 섞다
- [ ] monster — 괴물
- [ ] orange — 주황색, 오렌지
- [ ] purple — 보라색
- [ ] red — 빨간색
- [ ] white — 흰색
- [ ] yellow — 노란색

· Unit 9 ·
Food from the Farm

- [ ] bread   빵
- [ ] cheese   치즈
- [ ] come from
      ~에서 나오다, 생산되다
- [ ] corn   옥수수
- [ ] cow   젖소
- [ ] dinner   저녁 식사
- [ ] egg   달걀
- [ ] else   또 다른
- [ ] farm   농장
- [ ] food   음식, 식량
- [ ] grow   자라다
- [ ] hen   암탉
- [ ] ketchup   케첩
- [ ] milk   우유
- [ ] tomato   토마토
- [ ] what   무엇, 어떤
- [ ] wheat   밀
- [ ] where   어디에서

· Unit 10 ·
Let's Travel

- [ ] across
      ~을 건너서/가로질러

- [ ] boat   배, 보트
- [ ] bus   버스
- [ ] drive   운전하다
- [ ] fly   날다, 비행하다
- [ ] plane   비행기
- [ ] railroad   기찻길
- [ ] river   강
- [ ] road   도로, 길
- [ ] row   노를 젓다
- [ ] sail   항해하다
- [ ] take
      (교통수단을) 타다, 이용하다
- [ ] train   기차
- [ ] travel   여행하다

· Unit 11 ·
We Are Friends

- [ ] back   되받아, 뒤로
- [ ] book   책
- [ ] but   하지만, 그러나
- [ ] eat   먹다
- [ ] fight   싸우다
- [ ] friends   친구
- [ ] know   알다, 알고 있다
- [ ] lunch   점심 식사
- [ ] share   같이 쓰다, 나누다
- [ ] smile   미소 짓다; 미소

- [ ] sometimes   가끔, 때때로
- [ ] soon   곧
- [ ] talk   이야기하다
- [ ] then   그러면
- [ ] together   함께, 같이
- [ ] toy   장난감
- [ ] who   누구

· Unit 12 ·
Touching Animals

- [ ] cool   시원한
- [ ] hedgehog   고슴도치
- [ ] iguana   이구아나
- [ ] jungle   정글, 밀림
- [ ] monkey   원숭이
- [ ] rough   거친
- [ ] smooth   매끈한
- [ ] snake   뱀
- [ ] soft   부드러운
- [ ] something   어떤 것
- [ ] spiky   뾰족한
- [ ] touch   만지다
- [ ] turtle   거북이

1.2

미국교과서 리딩

READING

Workbook & Answer Key

길벗스쿨

READING

미국교과서 리딩

LEVEL 1 ②

Workbook

길벗스쿨

I Like the Rain

Word Review

Ⓐ Match and trace.

1.

2.

3.

4.

boots

rain

socks

splash

Ⓑ Look and circle.

1.  raincoat rain

2.  shirt boots

Sentence Review

A Choose and write.

put	splash	socks

1.  I put on my socks .

2. I _____ on my shirt.

3. I _____ in the rain.

B Unscramble and write.

1. too. put on my boots, I

→ I put on my boots, too.

2. in the rain. jump I

→

3. is raining. It

→

Spring Is Here

Word Review

A Match and trace.

1.

flower

2.

bird

3.

frog

4.

stream

B Look and circle.

1.  flower

snow

2.  melt

frog

Sentence Review

A **Choose and write.**

running	singing	flowers

1. The _____ are blooming.

2. The streams are _____ .

3. The birds are _____ .

B **Unscramble and write.**

1. [is] [Spring] [here.]

→ _____

2. [jumping.] [are] [The frogs]

→ _____

3. [is] [The snow] [melting.]

→ _____

They Go Together

Word Review

A Match and trace.

1.

2.

3.

4.

wear

mittens

chopsticks

shoes

B Look and circle.

1.

mittens

pair

2.

together

wear

Sentence Review

A Choose and write.

together	Chopsticks	pair

1. Mittens are a _____ .

2. _____ are a pair, too.

3. We wear them _____ .

B Unscramble and write.

1. | are | Shoes | a pair. |

→ _____

2. | go | always | together. | They |

→ _____

3. | them | use | We | together. |

→ _____

Word Review

A Match and trace.

1.

nest

2.

fox

3.

den

4.

home

B Look and circle.

1.

fox

hive

2.

web

den

Sentence Review

A Choose and write.

home	fox	hive

1. A [   ] is home to a bee.

2. A nest is [   ] to a bird.

3. A den is home to a [   ] .

B Unscramble and write.

1. | is | A web | home | to a spider. |

   ➔ _____

2. | in a nest. | lives | A bird |

   ➔ _____

3. | A bee | in a hive | lives |

   ➔ _____

The City and the Country

Word Review

A **Match and trace.**

1.

car

2.

tree

3.

building

4.

country

B **Look and circle.**

1.
city
country

2.
building
hill

Sentence Review

A Choose and write.

| cars | buildings | country |

1. Farmer Bob lives in the _____ .

2. There are many _____ .

3. There are _____ .

B Unscramble and write.

1. | can | fast. | move | He |

→ _____

2. | the country. | likes | He |

→ _____

3. | There | trees. | are | many |

→ _____

Word Review

(A) Match and trace.

1.

messy

2.

book

3.

floor

4.

pencil

(B) Look and circle.

1.

chair

pencil

2.

book

room

Sentence Review

A Choose and write.

chair	like	floor

1. I _____ my messy room.

2. I like books on the _____ .

3. I like pencils on the _____ .

B Unscramble and write.

1. | pants | the bed. | like | I | on |

→ _____

2. | My mom | it. | like | does not |

→ _____

3. | my room. | everything | in | like | I |

→ _____

A Bad Dream

Word Review

Ⓐ Match and trace.

1.

2.

3.

4.

lion

jungle

bear

alligator

Ⓑ Look and circle.

1.

cave

lion

2.

river

bear

Sentence Review

A **Choose and write.**

alligator	jungle	swim

1. I run in the _____ .

2. I meet a hungry _____ .

3. I _____ in a river.

B **Unscramble and write.**

1. | the air. | fly | I | in |

   →

2. | in | walk | I | a cave. |

   →

3. | meet | I | a hungry | bear. |

   →

Color Magician

Word Review

Ⓐ Match and trace.

1.

    mix

2.

    red

3.

    blue

4.

    yellow

Ⓑ Look and circle.

1.

    blue

    magician

2.

    purple

    yellow

Sentence Review

A Choose and write.

blue	black	mix

1. I mix red and _____ .
That makes purple.

2. I _____ yellow and blue.
That makes green.

3. I mix _____ and white.
That makes gray.

B Unscramble and write.

1. | orange. | makes | That |

→ _____

2. | the colors. | all | I | mix |

→ _____

3. | a monster! | I | Oh, | made |

→ _____

Food from the Farm

Word Review

A Match and trace.

1.

tomato

2.

wheat

3.

milk

4.

grow

B Look and circle.

1.

farm

milk

2.

bread

tomato

Sentence Review

A **Choose and write.**

Ketchup	Milk	wheat

1. _____ comes from tomatoes.

2. Bread comes from _____ .

3. _____ comes from cows.

B **Unscramble and write.**

1. | food | does | Where | come from? |

➝ _____

2. | on the farm. | Hens | cows | and | live |

➝ _____

3. | come from | Eggs | hens. |

➝ _____

Word Review

A Match and trace.

1.

railroad

2.

train

3.

boat

4.

drive

B Look and circle.

1.

road

boat

2.

sail

train

Sentence Review

A **Choose and write.**

railroad	take	boat

1. We take a _____ . Row! Row!

2. Let's run on the _____ .

3. We _____ a plane. Zoom! Zoom!

B **Unscramble and write.**

1. | take | We | a bus. |

   ➜ _____

2. | Let's | across the river. | sail |

   ➜ _____

3. | on the road. | drive | Let's |

   ➜ _____

We Are Friends

Word Review

A Match and trace.

1.

share

2.

smile

3.

fight

4.

toys

B Look and circle.

1.

fight

talk

2.

toys

friends

Sentence Review

A **Choose and write.**

share	toys	lunch

1. We share _____ .

2. We eat _____ together.

3. We don't _____ books.

B **Unscramble and write.**

1. | we | Then, | talk | together. |

→ _____

2. | together. | We | eat | don't |

→ _____

3. | at me. | She | smiles |

→ _____

Touching Animals

Word Review

A Match and trace.

1.

    smooth

2.

    rough

3.

    spiky

4.

    cool

B Look and circle.

1.

    spiky

    touch

2.

    soft

    rough

Sentence Review

A **Choose and write.**

smooth	touch	spiky

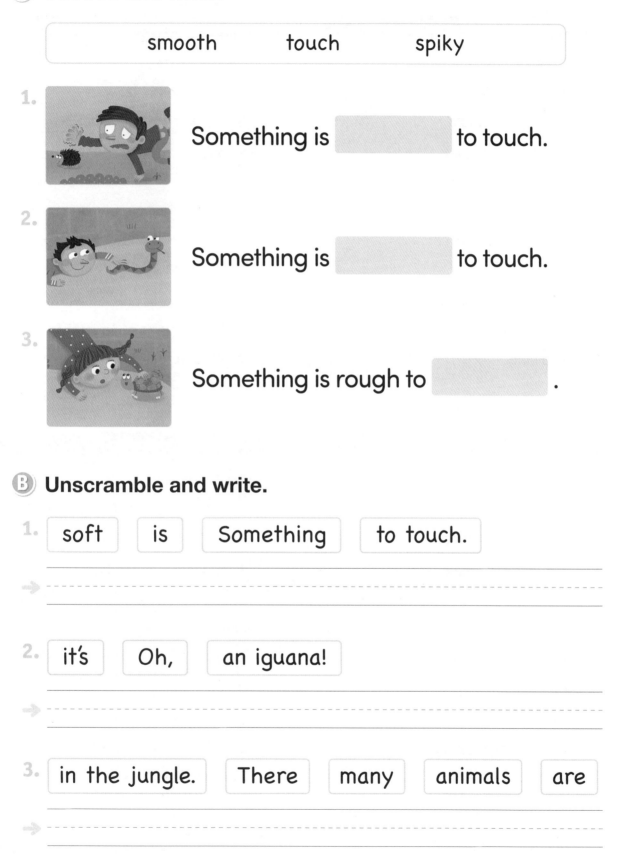

1. Something is _____ to touch.

2. Something is _____ to touch.

3. Something is rough to _____ .

B **Unscramble and write.**

1. | soft | is | Something | to touch. |

➡ _____

2. | it's | Oh, | an iguana! |

➡ _____

3. | in the jungle. | There | many | animals | are |

➡ _____

Workbook | 워크북 정답

Unit 1. I Like the Rain

■ Words Review

A **1.** splash **2.** socks

3. boots **4.** rain

B **1.** raincoat **2.** shirt

■ Sentences Review

A **1.** socks **2.** put

3. splash

B **1.** I put on my boots, too.

2. I jump in the rain.

3. It is raining.

Unit 2. Spring Is Here

■ Words Review

A **1.** frog **2.** bird

3. flower **4.** stream

B **1.** snow **2.** melt

■ Sentences Review

A **1.** flowers **2.** running

3. singing

B **1.** Spring is here.

2. The frogs are jumping.

3. The snow is melting.

Unit 3. They Go Together

■ Words Review

A **1.** chopsticks **2.** wear

3. mittens **4.** shoes

B **1.** pair **2.** together

■ Sentences Review

A **1.** pair **2.** Chopsticks

3. together

B **1.** Shoes are a pair.

2. They always go together.

3. We use them together.

Unit 4. Animal Homes

■ Words Review

A **1.** home **2.** fox

3. nest **4.** den

B **1.** hive **2.** web

■ Sentences Review

A **1.** hive **2.** home

3. fox

B **1.** A web is home to a spider.

2. A bird lives in a nest.

3. A bee lives in a hive.

Unit 5. The City and the Country

■ Words Review

Ⓐ **1.** car **2.** building

3. tree **4.** country

Ⓑ **1.** city **2.** hill

■ Sentences Review

Ⓐ **1.** country **2.** cars

3. buildings

Ⓑ **1.** He can move fast.

2. He likes the country.

3. There are many trees.

Unit 6. My Messy Room

■ Words Review

Ⓐ **1.** book **2.** pencil

3. messy **4.** floor

Ⓑ **1.** chair **2.** room

■ Sentences Review

Ⓐ **1.** like **2.** chair

3. floor

Ⓑ **1.** I like pants on the bed.

2. My mom does not like it.

3. I like everything in my room.

Unit 7. A Bad Dream

■ Words Review

Ⓐ **1.** bear **2.** lion

3. alligator **4.** jungle

Ⓑ **1.** cave **2.** river

■ Sentences Review

Ⓐ **1.** jungle **2.** alligator

3. swim

Ⓑ **1.** I fly in the air.

2. I walk in a cave.

3. I meet a hungry bear.

Unit 8. Color Magician

■ Words Review

Ⓐ **1.** red **2.** mix

3. yellow **4.** blue

Ⓑ **1.** magician **2.** purple

■ Sentences Review

Ⓐ **1.** blue **2.** mix

3. black

Ⓑ **1.** That makes orange.

2. I mix all the colors.

3. Oh, I made a monster!

Unit 9. Food from the Farm

■ Words Review

Ⓐ **1.** wheat   **2.** tomato

    3. milk   **4.** grow

Ⓑ **1.** farm   **2.** bread

■ Sentences Review

Ⓐ **1.** Ketchup   **2.** wheat

    3. Milk

Ⓑ **1.** Where does food come from?

    2. Hens and cows live on the farm.

    3. Eggs come from hens.

Unit 10. Let's Travel

■ Words Review

Ⓐ **1.** train   **2.** boat

    3. drive   **4.** railroad

Ⓑ **1.** road   **2.** sail

■ Sentences Review

Ⓐ **1.** boat   **2.** railroad

    3. take

Ⓑ **1.** We take a bus.

    2. Let's sail across the river.

    3. Let's drive on the road.

Unit 11. We Are Friends

■ Words Review

Ⓐ **1.** toys   **2.** share

    3. fight   **4.** smile

Ⓑ **1.** talk   **2.** friends

■ Sentences Review

Ⓐ **1.** toys   **2.** lunch

    3. share

Ⓑ **1.** Then, we talk together.

    2. We don't eat together.

    3. She smiles at me.

Unit 12. Touching Animals

■ Words Review

Ⓐ **1.** spiky   **2.** rough

    3. smooth   **4.** cool

Ⓑ **1.** touch   **2.** soft

■ Sentences Review

Ⓐ **1.** spiky   **2.** smooth

    3. touch

Ⓑ **1.** Something is soft to touch.

    2. Oh, it's an iguana!

    3. There are many animals in the jungle.

미국교과서 리딩 READING

LEVEL 1 ②

Answer Key

길벗스쿨

■ **Get Ready** p.10

■ **Key Words** 단어를 듣고, 알맞은 사진을 가리키세요.

rain 비; 비가 오다   shirt 셔츠   socks 양말

raincoat 비옷   boots 장화   splash 첨벙거리다

■ **Quick Check** 알맞은 단어에 동그라미 하세요.

socks   shirt   rain   boots

■ **Key Sentence**

I put on my socks. (나는 양말을 신어요.)

듣고 따라 말한 후 알맞게 연결하세요.

I put on my shirt. (나는 셔츠를 입어요.) ⓒ

I put on my raincoat. (나는 비옷을 입어요.) ⓑ

I put on my boots. (나는 장화를 신어요.) ⓓ

I put on my pants. (나는 바지를 입어요.) ⓐ

■ **Quick Check** 알맞은 단어에 동그라미 하고 쓰세요.

I put on my boots. (나는 장화를 신어요.)

■ **Now You Read** p.12

나는 비를 좋아해요

비가 와요.
지루해요.

아, 내게 좋은 생각이 있어요!
나는 셔츠를 입어요.
나는 양말을 신어요.

나는 비옷을 입어요.
나는 장화도 신어요.

나는 빗속에서 점프해요.
나는 빗속에서 첨벙거려요.

그래요, 나는 비를 좋아해요!

■ **Pop Quiz**

여자아이의 비옷은 무슨 색인가요?   노란색(yellow)

■ **Check Up** p.14

■ **Comprehension** 다음을 읽고 알맞은 것에 체크하세요.

1. 이것은 _____에 대한 이야기예요.
   ☑ 비 오는 날   ☐ 맑은 날

2. 나는 빗속에서 _____.
   ☐ 날아요   ☑ 점프해요

3. 눈이 와요.   False

4. 나는 비를 좋아해요.   True

■ **Sentence** 그림을 보고 문장에 알맞은 단어에 동그라미 하세요.

1. It is raining. (비가 와요.)

2. I put on my socks. (나는 양말을 신어요.)

3. I splash in the rain. (나는 빗속에서 첨벙거려요.)

■ **Word** 퍼즐을 완성하세요.

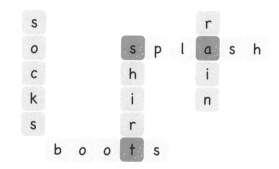

■ **Wrap-up** 단어를 읽고, 빈칸에 해당하는 것에 동그라미 하세요.

I put on my _____. (나는 ~을 입어요(신어요).)

shirt (셔츠)

boots (장화)

raincoat (비옷)

socks (양말)

Spring Is Here 봄이 왔어요

Get Ready p.16

■ Key Words 단어를 듣고, 알맞은 사진을 가리키세요.

snow 눈   melt 녹다   flower 꽃

stream 시냇물   bird 새   frog 개구리

■ Quick Check 알맞은 단어에 동그라미 하세요.

flower   frog   bird   stream

■ Key Sentence

The snow is melting. (눈이 녹고 있어요.)

듣고 따라 말한 후 알맞게 연결하세요.

The flowers are blooming. (꽃이 피고 있어요.) ⓓ

The streams are running. (시냇물이 흐르고 있어요.) ⓑ

The birds are singing. (새가 노래하고 있어요.) ⓐ

The frogs are jumping. (개구리가 뛰고 있어요.) ⓒ

■ Quick Check 알맞은 단어에 동그라미 하고 쓰세요.

The birds are singing. (새가 노래하고 있어요.)

Now You Read p.18

봄이 왔어요

봄이 왔어요.
눈이 녹고 있어요.

봄이 왔어요.
꽃이 피고 있어요.

봄이 왔어요.
시냇물이 흐르고 있어요.

봄이 왔어요.
새가 노래하고 있어요.

봄이 왔어요.
개구리가 뛰고 있어요.

봄이 왔어요.
우리도 노래하고 있어요!
우리도 뛰고 있어요!

■ Pop Quiz

개구리가 몇 마리 보이나요?   네 마리(four frogs)

Check Up p.20

■ Comprehension 다음을 읽고 알맞은 것에 체크하세요.

1. 이것은 _____에 대한 이야기예요.
☑ 봄   □ 겨울

2. 눈이 _____ 있어요.
□ 피고   ☑ 녹고

3. 여름이 왔어요.   False

4. 우리도 노래하고 있어요.   True

■ Sentence 그림을 보고 문장에 알맞은 단어에 동그라미 하세요.

1. The birds are singing. (새가 노래하고 있어요.)

2. The flowers are blooming. (꽃이 피고 있어요.)

3. Spring is here. (봄이 왔어요.)

■ Word 단어를 찾아 동그라미 하세요.

s	f	a	b	c	h	k	p
n	r	q	g	f	a	k	e
o	o	r	u	i	p	n	l
w	g	s	t	r	e	a	m
q	h	m	c	d	e	g	y
f	l	o	w	e	r	s	e

■ Wrap-up 관계 있는 것끼리 연결하고 알맞은 단어를 쓰세요.

1. ⓒ The snow is melting. (눈이 녹고 있어요.)

2. ⓐ The frogs are jumping. (개구리가 뛰고 있어요.)

3. ⓑ The birds are singing. (새가 노래하고 있어요.)

They Go Together 그것들은 함께 다녀요

Get Ready
p.22

■ Key Words 단어를 듣고, 알맞은 사진을 가리키세요.

pair 한 쌍   wear 입다, 신다   together 함께

shoes 신발   mittens 손모아장갑   chopsticks 젓가락

■ Quick Check 알맞은 단어에 동그라미 하세요.

chopsticks   mittens   shoes   wear

■ Key Sentence

Socks are a pair. (양말은 한 쌍이에요.)

듣고 따라 말한 후 알맞게 연결하세요.

Shoes are a pair. (신발은 한 쌍이에요.) ⓑ

Chopsticks are a pair. (젓가락은 한 쌍이에요.) ⓒ

Mittens are a pair. (손모아장갑은 한 쌍이에요.) ⓓ

Gloves are a pair. (장갑은 한 쌍이에요.) ⓐ

■ Quick Check 알맞은 단어에 동그라미 하고 쓰세요.

Shoes are a pair. (신발은 한 쌍이에요.)

Now You Read
p.24

그것들은 함께 다녀요

한 쌍인 것을 찾을 수 있나요?

양말이 한 쌍이에요.
우리는 그것들을 함께 신어요.

신발이 한 쌍이에요.
우리는 그것들을 함께 신어요.

벙어리장갑이 한 쌍이에요.
우리는 그것들을 함께 껴요.

아, 하나 더!
젓가락도 한 쌍이에요.
우리는 그것들을 함께 사용해요.

그것들은 언제나 함께 다녀요.

■ Pop Quiz

바깥의 날씨는 어떤가요?
눈이 오고 있어요. (It is snowing.)

Check Up
p.26

■ Comprehension 다음을 읽고 알맞은 것에 체크하세요.

1. 이것은 _____ 에 대한 이야기예요.
   □ 신발   ☑ 한 쌍

2. _____는(은) 한 쌍이에요.
   □ 셔츠   ☑ 손모아장갑

3. 책상은 한 쌍이에요.   False

4. 우리는 신발을 함께 신어요.   True

■ Sentence 그림을 보고 문장에 알맞은 단어에 동그라미 하세요.

1. Socks are a pair. (양말은 한 쌍이에요.)

2. Chopsticks are a pair. (젓가락은 한 쌍이에요.)

3. We wear them together. (우리는 그것들을 함께 껴요.)

■ Word 퍼즐을 완성하세요.

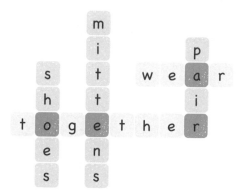

■ Wrap-up 단어를 읽고, 빈칸에 해당하는 것에 동그라미 하세요.

_____ are a pair. (~은 한 쌍이에요.)

Socks (양말)   Mittens (손모아장갑)

Boots (장화)   Shoes (신발)

Chopsticks (젓가락)

Get Ready   p.28

- **Key Words** 단어를 듣고, 알맞은 사진을 가리키세요.

  hive 벌집   home 집   nest 둥지
  den (야생 동물이 사는) 굴   fox 여우   web 거미줄

- **Quick Check** 알맞은 단어에 동그라미 하세요.

  hive   nest   web   home

- **Key Sentence**

  A hive is home to a bee. (벌집은 벌에게 집이에요.)

듣고 따라 말한 후 알맞게 연결하세요.

A nest is home to a bird. (둥지는 새에게 집이에요.) ⓐ
A den is home to a fox. (굴은 여우에게 집이에요.) ⓒ
A web is home to a spider. (거미줄은 거미에게 집이에요.) ⓑ
A stream is home to a frog. (시냇물은 개구리에게 집이에요.) ⓓ

- **Quick Check** 알맞은 단어에 동그라미 하고 쓰세요.

  A web is home to a spider. (거미줄은 거미에게 집이에요.)

Now You Read   p.30

동물들의 집

벌집은 벌에게 집이에요.
벌은 벌집에서 살아요.

둥지는 새에게 집이에요.
새는 둥지에서 살아요.

굴은 여우에게 집이에요.
여우는 굴에서 살아요.

거미줄은 거미에게 집이에요.
거미는 거미줄에서 살아요.

- **Pop Quiz**

  둥지에 새 몇 마리가 있나요?   네 마리(four birds)

Check Up   p.32

- **Comprehension** 다음을 읽고 알맞은 것에 체크하세요.

1. 이것은 _____에 대한 이야기예요.
   ☑ 동물의 집   ☐ 벌과 새

2. 벌은 _____에서 살아요.
   ☐ 거미줄   ☑ 벌집

3. 여우는 굴에서 살아요.   True

4. 거미줄은 새에게 집이에요.   False

- **Sentence** 그림을 보고 문장에 알맞은 단어에 동그라미 하세요.

1. A den is home to a fox. (굴은 여우에게 집이에요.)
2. A hive is home to a bee. (벌집은 벌에게 집이에요.)
3. A bird lives in a nest. (새는 둥지에서 살아요.)

- **Word** 단어를 찾아 동그라미 하세요.

n	e	s	t	o	n	q	w
a	m	d	v	m	e	y	t
d	p	e	h	i	v	e	b
e	x	c	o	m	n	e	t
n	v	m	m	q	a	b	e
c	d	f	e	e	y	t	b

- **Wrap-up** 관계 있는 것끼리 연결하고 알맞은 단어를 쓰세요.

1. ⓒ A bird lives in a nest. (새는 둥지에서 살아요.)
2. ⓑ A spider lives in a web. (거미는 거미줄에서 살아요.)
3. ⓐ A fox lives in a den. (여우는 굴에서 살아요.)

Get Ready   p.34

■ **Key Words** 단어를 듣고, 알맞은 사진을 가리키세요.

country 시골   tree 나무   hill 언덕

city 도시   building 빌딩   car 자동차

■ **Quick Check** 알맞은 단어에 동그라미 하세요.

city   country   building   tree

■ **Key Sentence**

There are hills. (언덕들이 있어요.)

듣고 따라 말한 후 알맞게 연결하세요.

There are many trees. (나무가 많이 있어요.) ⓑ

There are buildings. (빌딩이 있어요.) ⓐ

There are many cars. (자동차가 많이 있어요.) ⓓ

There are birds. (새가 있어요.) ⓒ

■ **Quick Check** 알맞은 단어에 동그라미 하고 쓰세요.

There are buildings. (빌딩이 있어요.)

Now You Read   p.36

도시와 시골

농부 밥은 시골에 살아요.
그는 시골을 좋아해요.

언덕이 있어요.
나무가 많이 있어요.
그는 신선한 과일을 먹을 수 있어요.

피터는 도시에 살아요.
그는 도시를 좋아해요.

빌딩이 있어요.
자동차가 많이 있어요.
그는 빨리 이동할 수 있어요.

■ **Pop Quiz**

농부 밥은 무엇을 먹고 있나요?   사과(an apple)

Check Up   p.38

■ **Comprehension** 다음을 읽고 알맞은 것에 체크하세요.

1. 이것은 _____에 대한 이야기예요.
   □ 학교   ☑ 도시와 시골

2. 피터는 _____에 살아요.
   □ 시골   ☑ 도시

3. 도시에는 언덕이 많이 있어요.   False

4. 농부 밥은 신선한 과일을 먹을 수 있어요.   True

■ **Sentence** 그림을 보고 문장에 알맞은 단어에 동그라미 하세요.

1. There are many cars. (자동차가 많이 있어요.)

2. There are buildings. (빌딩이 있어요.)

3. He can move fast. (그는 빨리 이동할 수 있어요.)

■ **Word** 퍼즐을 완성하세요.

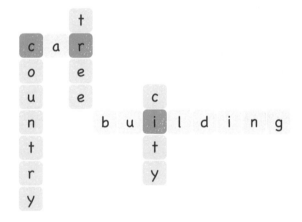

■ **Wrap-up** 그림을 보고 관련 있는 곳에 연결하세요.

1. country (시골) - hills (언덕), many trees (많은 나무),
   eat fresh fruits (신선한 과일을 먹다)

2. city (도시) - many cars (많은 자동차), buildings (빌딩),
   move fast (빨리 이동하다)

Get Ready
p.40

■ Key Words 단어를 듣고, 알맞은 사진을 가리키세요.

room 방   book 책   chair 의자

pencil 연필   floor 바닥   messy 지저분한, 엉망인

■ Quick Check 알맞은 단어에 동그라미 하세요.

room   book   pencil   chair

■ Key Sentence

I like pants on the bed. (나는 침대 위에 있는 바지가 좋아요.)

듣고 따라 말한 후 알맞게 연결하세요.

I like books on the chair. (나는 의자 위에 있는 책이 좋아요.) ⓐ

I like shirts on the desk. (나는 책상 위에 있는 셔츠가 좋아요.) ⓑ

I like pencils on the floor. (나는 바닥에 있는 연필이 좋아요.) ⓓ

I like socks on the door. (나는 문 위에 있는 양말이 좋아요.) ⓒ

■ Quick Check 알맞은 단어에 동그라미 하고 쓰세요.

I like pencils on the desk.
(나는 책상 위에 있는 연필이 좋아요.)

Now You Read
p.42

지저분한 내 방

나는 내 방이 좋아요.
나는 내 방에 있는 모든 것이 좋아요.

나는 침대 위에 있는 바지가 좋아요.
나는 의자 위에 있는 책이 좋아요.

나는 책상 위에 있는 셔츠들이 좋아요.
나는 바닥에 있는 연필이 좋아요.

나는 지저분한 내 방이 좋아요.
하지만 우리 엄마는 내 방을 좋아하지 않아요.
엄마는 내 방이 깨끗하길 원해요.

■ Pop Quiz

공은 어디에 있나요?   바닥(on the floor)

Check Up
p.44

■ Comprehension 다음을 읽고 알맞은 것에 체크하세요.

1. 이것은 _____에 대한 이야기예요.
   □ 우리 엄마   ☑ 지저분한 내 방

2. 나는 내 _____에 있는 모든 것이 좋아요.
   ☑ 방   □ 책상

3. 우리 엄마는 내 지저분한 방을 좋아해요.   False

4. 나는 침대 위에 있는 바지가 좋아요.   True

■ Sentence 그림을 보고 문장에 알맞은 단어에 동그라미 하세요.

1. I like shirts on the desk. (나는 책상 위에 있는 셔츠가 좋아요.)

2. I like books on the chair. (나는 의자 위에 있는 책이 좋아요.)

3. I like my messy room. (나는 지저분한 내 방이 좋아요.)

■ Word 단어를 찾아 동그라미 하세요.

a	e	i	e	o	h	v	m
c	s	j	r	l	u	b	e
h	r	o	o	k	c	v	s
a	s	h	o	r	p	m	s
i	n	p	m	q	d	g	y
r	f	f	l	o	o	r	c

■ Wrap-up 그림을 보고 알맞은 단어를 쓰세요.

1. I like books on the chair. (나는 의자 위에 있는 책이 좋아요.)

2. I like pants on the bed. (나는 침대 위에 있는 바지가 좋아요.)

3. I like pencils on the floor. (나는 바닥에 있는 연필이 좋아요.)

4. I like shirts on the desk. (나는 책상 위에 있는 셔츠가 좋아요.)

UNIT 7 · A Bad Dream 나쁜 꿈

Get Ready · p.46

■ Key Words 단어를 듣고, 알맞은 사진을 가리키세요.

cave 동굴   bear 곰   jungle 정글

lion 사자   river 강   alligator 악어

■ Quick Check 알맞은 단어에 동그라미 하세요.

cave   bear   lion   river

■ Key Sentence

I fly in the air. (나는 하늘을 날아요.)

듣고 따라 말한 후 알맞게 연결하세요.

I walk in a cave. (나는 동굴에서 걸어요.) ⓒ

I run in the jungle. (나는 정글에서 뛰어요.) ⓐ

I swim in a river. (나는 강에서 수영해요.) ⓑ

I jump in the rain. (나는 빗속에서 점프해요.) ⓓ

■ Quick Check 알맞은 단어에 동그라미 하고 쓰세요.

I swim in a river. (나는 강에서 수영해요.)

Now You Read · p.48

나쁜 꿈

나는 하늘을 날아요.
나는 배고픈 독수리를 만나요. "도와주세요!"

나는 동굴에서 걸어요.
나는 배고픈 곰을 만나요. "도와주세요!"

나는 정글에서 뛰어요.
나는 배고픈 사자를 만나요. "도와주세요!"

나는 강에서 수영해요.
나는 배고픈 악어를 만나요. "도와주세요!"

도와주세요! 도와주세요!
오, 그것은 단지 나쁜 꿈이었어요.

■ Pop Quiz

남자아이의 셔츠에 무슨 모양이 있나요?   별(a star)

Check Up · p.50

■ Comprehension 다음을 읽고 알맞은 것에 체크하세요.

1. 이것은 _____에 대한 이야기예요.
   ☑ 나쁜 꿈   ☐ 배고픈 곰

2. 꿈속에서 나는 _____ 독수리를 만나요.
   ☐ 행복한   ☑ 배고픈

3. 꿈속에서 나는 정글에서 뛰어요.   True

4. 꿈속에서 나는 배고픈 개구리를 만나요.   False

■ Sentence 그림을 보고 문장에 알맞은 단어에 동그라미 하세요.

1. I walk in a cave. (나는 동굴에서 걸어요.)
2. I fly in the air. (나는 하늘을 날아요.)
3. I meet a hungry lion. (나는 배고픈 사자를 만나요.)

■ Word 퍼즐을 완성하세요.

■ Wrap-up 문장을 읽고 해당하는 그림에 번호를 쓰세요.

(꿈속에서)

3. I meet a hungry lion. (나는 배고픈 사자를 만나요.)

4. I meet a hungry alligator. (나는 배고픈 악어를 만나요.)

1. I meet a hungry eagle. (나는 배고픈 독수리를 만나요.)

2. I meet a hungry bear. (나는 배고픈 곰을 만나요.)

- **Key Words** 단어를 듣고, 알맞은 사진을 가리키세요.

  mix 섞다　　　 red 빨간색　　　 blue 파란색

  yellow 노란색　　 green 초록색　　 black 검은색

- **Quick Check** 알맞은 단어에 동그라미 하세요.

  blue　　　 black　　　 green　　　 mix

- **Key Sentence**

  I mix red and blue. (나는 빨간색과 파란색을 섞어요.)

  듣고 따라 말한 후 알맞게 연결하세요.

  I mix yellow and blue. (나는 노란색과 파란색을 섞어요.) **ⓑ**
  I mix red and yellow. (나는 빨간색과 노란색을 섞어요.) **ⓐ**
  I mix black and white. (나는 검은색과 흰색을 섞어요.) **ⓓ**
  I mix all the colors. (나는 모든 색을 섞어요.) **ⓒ**

- **Quick Check** 알맞은 단어에 동그라미 하고 쓰세요.

  I mix red and yellow. (나는 빨간색과 노란색을 섞어요.)

색 마술사

나는 색 마술사예요.
나는 색을 만들어요.

나는 빨간색과 파란색을 섞어요.
그것은 보라색을 만들어요.

나는 노란색과 파란색을 섞어요.
그것은 초록색을 만들어요.

나는 빨간색과 노란색을 섞어요.
그것은 주황색을 만들어요.

나는 검은색과 흰색을 섞어요.
그것은 회색을 만들어요.

나는 모든 색을 섞어요.
오, 내가 괴물을 만들었어요!

괴물은 무슨 색인가요?　　　　　　　　 검은색(black)

- **Comprehension** 다음을 읽고 알맞은 것에 체크하세요.

1. 이것은 _____에 대한 이야기예요.
　☑ 색　　　　　　　　　 □ 모양

2. 나는 색을 _____.
　☑ 만들어요　　　　　　 □ 그려요

3. 나는 책 마술사예요.　　　　　　　　 False

4. 내가 괴물을 만들었어요.　　　　　　 True

- **Sentence** 그림을 보고 문장에 알맞은 단어에 동그라미 하세요.

1. I mix yellow and blue. (나는 노란색과 파란색을 섞어요.)
2. I mix black and white. (나는 검은색과 흰색을 섞어요.)
3. That makes orange. (그것은 주황색을 만들어요.)

- **Word** 단어를 찾아 동그라미 하세요.

g	r	e	e	n	o	w	d
a	w	y	d	h	f	c	r
b	l	a	c	k	y	d	a
l	o	n	e	f	s	c	d
u	p	g	r	x	b	v	x
e	y	e	l	l	o	w	p

- **Wrap-up** 그림을 보고 알맞은 단어를 쓰세요.

1. I mix yellow and blue. That makes green.
(나는 노란색과 파란색을 섞어요. 그것은 초록색을 만들어요.)

2. I mix black and white. That makes gray.
(나는 검은색과 흰색을 섞어요. 그것은 회색을 만들어요.)

3. I mix red and blue. That makes purple.
(나는 빨간색과 파란색을 섞어요. 그것은 보라색을 만들어요.)

4. I mix red and yellow. That makes orange.
(나는 빨간색과 노란색을 섞어요. 그것은 주황색을 만들어요.)

Get Ready

p.58

■ Key Words 단어를 듣고, 알맞은 사진을 가리키세요.

bread 빵   wheat 밀   tomato 토마토

grow 자라다   farm 농장   milk 우유

■ Quick Check 알맞은 단어에 동그라미 하세요.

bread   wheat   milk   farm

■ Key Sentence

Bread comes from wheat. (빵은 밀에서 나와요.)

듣고 따라 말한 후 알맞게 연결하세요.

Ketchup comes from tomatoes. (케첩은 토마토에서 나와요.) ⓒ

Eggs come from hens. (달걀은 암탉에서 나와요.) ⓑ

Milk comes from cows. (우유는 젖소에서 나와요.) ⓓ

Cheese comes from cows. (치즈는 젖소에서 나와요.) ⓐ

■ Quick Check 알맞은 단어에 동그라미 하고 쓰세요.

Eggs come from hens. (달걀은 암탉에서 나와요.)

Now You Read

p.60

농장에서 온 음식

점심시간이에요!

음식은 어디에서 올까요?

빵은 밀에서 나와요. (빵은 밀로 만들어요.)

케첩은 토마토에서 나와요. (케첩은 토마토로 만들어요.)

밀과 토마토는 농장에서 자라요.

달걀은 암탉에서 나와요.

우유는 젖소에서 나오죠.

암탉과 젖소는 농장에서 살아요.

농장에서 또 무엇이 나올까요?

■ Pop Quiz

어떤 동물들을 볼 수 있나요? 암탉과 젖소(hens and cows)

Check Up

p.62

■ Comprehension 다음을 읽고 알맞은 것에 체크하세요.

1. 이것은 _____에 대한 이야기예요.

  ☐ 동물을 위한 음식   ☑ 농장에서 온 음식

2. 밀과 토마토는 _____에서 자라요.

  ☑ 농장   ☐ 도시

3. 우유는 암탉에서 나와요.   False

4. 암탉과 젖소는 농장에서 살아요.   True

■ Sentence 그림을 보고 문장에 알맞은 단어에 동그라미 하세요.

1. Ketchup comes from tomatoes. (케첩은 토마토에서 나와요.)

2. Bread comes from wheat. (빵은 밀에서 나와요.)

3. Wheat and tomatoes grow on the farm.

  (밀과 토마토는 농장에서 자라요.)

■ Word 퍼즐을 완성하세요.

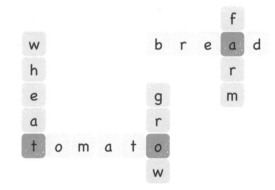

■ Wrap-up 관계 있는 것끼리 연결하고 알맞은 단어를 쓰세요.

1. ⓑ Ketchup comes from tomatoes.

  (케첩은 토마토에서 나와요.)

2. ⓐ Milk comes from cows. (우유는 젖소에서 나와요.)

3. ⓒ Bread comes from wheat. (빵은 밀에서 나와요.)

Get Ready p.64

■ **Key Words** 단어를 듣고, 알맞은 사진을 가리키세요.

boat 배, 보트   sail 항해하다   drive 운전하다
road 도로, 길   train 기차   railroad 기찻길

■ **Quick Check** 알맞은 단어에 동그라미 하세요.

train   road   drive   boat

■ **Key Sentence**

We take a boat. (우리는 배를 타.)

듣고 따라 말한 후 알맞게 연결하세요.
We take a bus. (우리는 버스를 타.) ⓒ
We take a plane. (우리는 비행기를 타.) ⓐ
We take a train. (우리는 기차를 타.) ⓓ
We take a car. (우리는 자동차를 타.) ⓑ

■ **Quick Check** 알맞은 단어에 동그라미 하고 쓰세요.

We take a bus. (우리는 버스를 타.)

Now You Read p.66

여행을 떠나자

우리는 배를 타. 노를 저어! 노를 저어!
강을 가로질러 항해하자.

우리는 버스를 타. 부릉! 부릉!
도로 위에서 운전하자.

우리는 비행기를 타. 슝! 슝!
하늘을 날자.

우리는 기차를 타. 칙칙폭폭!
기찻길 위에서 달려보자.

■ **Pop Quiz**

파란색 모자를 쓴 여자아이는 무엇을 하고 있나요?

운전(driving)

Check Up p.68

■ **Comprehension** 다음을 읽고 알맞은 것에 체크하세요.

1. 이것은 _____에 대한 이야기예요.
   ☑ 여행   □ 날씨

2. _____을 가로질러 항해하자.
   □ 하늘   ☑ 강

3. 우리는 비행기를 타.   True

4. 도로 위에서 날자.   False

■ **Sentence** 그림을 보고 문장에 알맞은 단어에 동그라미 하세요.

1. We take a boat. (우리는 배를 타.)
2. We take a bus. (우리는 버스를 타.)
3. Let's run on the railroad. (기찻길 위에서 달려보자.)

■ **Word** 단어를 찾아 동그라미 하세요.

t	o	g	o	b	t	f	s
r	p	r	t	i	d	v	a
a	q	s	r	c	m	x	i
i	s	g	o	r	l	m	l
n	x	d	a	w	h	f	m
a	b	c	d	r	i	v	e

■ **Wrap-up** 그림을 보고 알맞은 단어를 쓰세요.

1. We take a plane. Let's fly in the air.
   (우리는 비행기를 타. 하늘을 날자.)
2. We take a bus. Let's drive on the road.
   (우리는 버스를 타. 도로 위에서 운전하자.)
3. We take a boat. Let's sail across the river.
   (우리는 배를 타. 강을 가로질러 항해하자.)
4. We take a train. Let's run on the railroad.
   (우리는 기차를 타. 기찻길 위에서 달려보자.)

Get Ready   p.70

■ **Key Words** 단어를 듣고, 알맞은 사진을 가리키세요.

fight 싸우다   talk 이야기하다

share 같이 쓰다, 나누다   smile 미소 짓다

toys 장난감   friends 친구

■ **Quick Check** 알맞은 단어에 동그라미 하세요.

talk   smile   toys   friends

■ **Key Sentence**

We don't talk. (우리는 이야기하지 않아요.)

듣고 따라 말한 후 알맞게 연결하세요.

We share toys. (우리는 같이 장난감을 가지고 놀아요.) ⓐ

We eat lunch together. (우리는 같이 점심을 먹어요.) ⓓ

We don't share books. (우리는 같이 책을 보지 않아요.) ⓒ

We don't eat together. (우리는 같이 먹지 않아요.) ⓑ

■ **Quick Check** 알맞은 단어에 동그라미 하고 쓰세요.

We share toys. (우리는 같이 장난감을 가지고 놀아요.)

Now You Read   p.72

우리는 친구예요

가끔 우리는 싸워요.
그러면 우리는 이야기하지 않아요.
우리는 같이 책을 보지 않아요.
우리는 같이 먹지 않아요.

하지만 곧 그 애가 나에게 미소 지어요.
나도 똑같이 미소 지어요.

그러면 우리는 같이 이야기해요.
우리는 같이 장난감을 가지고 놀아요.
우리는 같이 점심을 먹어요.

우리가 누구인지 알아요?
맞아요. 우리는 친구예요!

■ **Pop Quiz**

몇 권의 책이 보이나요?   아홉 권(nine books)

Check Up   p.74

■ **Comprehension** 다음을 읽고 알맞은 것에 체크하세요.

1. 이것은 _____에 대한 이야기예요.
   □ 장난감   ☑ 친구

2. 가끔, 우리는 _____.
   ☑ 싸워요   □ 날아요

3. 우리는 친구예요.   True

4. 우리는 싸우지 않아요.   False

■ **Sentence** 그림을 보고 문장에 알맞은 단어에 동그라미 하세요.

1. We don't eat together. (우리는 같이 먹지 않아요.)
2. We share toys. (우리는 같이 장난감을 가지고 놀아요.)
3. She smiles at me. (그 애가 나에게 미소 지어요.)

■ **Word** 퍼즐을 완성하세요.

■ **Wrap-up** 그림을 보고 알맞은 표현을 쓰세요.

1. We talk together. (우리는 같이 이야기해요.) ↔
   We don't talk together. (우리는 같이 이야기하지 않아요.)

2. We share toys. (우리는 같이 장난감을 가지고 놀아요.) ↔
   We don't share toys. (우리는 같이 장난감을 가지고 놀지 않아요.)

3. We eat lunch together. (우리는 같이 점심을 먹어요.) ↔
   We don't eat lunch together.
   (우리는 같이 점심을 먹지 않아요.)

Get Ready

p.76

■ **Key Words** 단어를 듣고, 알맞은 사진을 가리키세요.

touch 만지다　　smooth 매끈한　　cool 시원한
rough 거친　　　soft 부드러운　　spiky 뾰족한

■ **Quick Check** 알맞은 단어에 동그라미 하세요.

smooth　　soft　　rough　　cool

■ **Key Sentence**

Something is smooth to touch.
(어떤 것은 만지면 매끄러워요.)

듣고 따라 말한 후 알맞게 연결하세요.

Something is cool to touch. (어떤 것은 만지면 시원해요.) **ⓐ**

Something is rough to touch. (어떤 것은 만지면 거칠어요.) **ⓒ**

Something is soft to touch. (어떤 것은 만지면 부드러워요.) **ⓑ**

Something is spiky to touch. (어떤 것은 만지면 뾰족해요.) **ⓓ**

■ **Quick Check** 알맞은 단어에 동그라미 하고 쓰세요.

Something is soft to touch. (어떤 것은 만지면 부드러워요.)

Now You Read

p.78

동물들 만지기

정글에는 많은 동물들이 있어요.

어떤 것은 만지면 매끄러워요.
앗, 그것은 뱀이에요!

어떤 것은 만지면 시원해요.
앗, 그것은 이구아나예요!

어떤 것은 만지면 거칠어요.
앗, 그것은 거북이예요!

어떤 것은 만지면 부드러워요.
앗, 그것은 원숭이예요!

어떤 것은 만지면 뾰족해요.
앗, 그것은 고슴도치예요!

■ **Pop Quiz**

아이들은 어떤 동물들을 만지고 있나요?
뱀, 이구아나, 거북이, 원숭이, 고슴도치(a snake, an iguana,
a turtle, a monkey, and a hedgehog)

Check Up

p.80

■ **Comprehension** 다음을 읽고 알맞은 것에 체크하세요.

1. 이것은 동물을 _____에 대한 이야기예요.
　　☐ 그리는 것　　　　☑ 만지는 것

2. 뱀은 만지면 _____.
　　☑ 매끄러워요　　　☐ 뜨거워요

3. 거북이는 만지면 뾰족해요.　　　　　　　False

4. 정글에는 많은 동물이 있어요.　　　　　　True

■ **Sentence** 그림을 보고 문장에 알맞은 단어에 동그라미 하세요.

1. Something is smooth to touch. (어떤 것은 만지면 매끄러워요.)

2. Something is soft to touch. (어떤 것은 만지면 부드러워요.)

3. It's a hedgehog! (그것은 고슴도치예요!)

■ **Word** 단어를 찾아 동그라미 하세요.

s	o	b	t	p	o	i	f
m	s	c	o	o	l	c	r
o	w	o	u	c	s	f	o
o	p	l	c	m	x	c	u
t	a	c	h	b	d	f	g
h	e	u	t	a	v	x	h

■ **Wrap-up** 그림을 보고 관계 있는 것끼리 연결하세요.

1. hedgehog (고슴도치) - spiky (뾰족한)

2. iguana (이구아나) - cool (시원한)

3. turtle (거북이) - rough (거친)

4. monkey (원숭이) - soft (부드러운)

5. snake (뱀) - smooth (매끈한)

미국교과서 READING Level 1 권별 리딩 주제

1권
1.1

1. Body Parts
2. My Brother
3. Family
4. My School
5. Animals
6. Seasons

7. Things in the Sky
8. Shapes
9. Clothes
10. Monsters
11. Jobs
12. Museum

2권
1.2

1. Rain
2. Spring
3. Things in Pairs
4. Animal Homes
5. Community
6 My Room

7. Bad Dream
8. Colors
9. Food
10. Transportation
11. Friends
12. Sense of Touch

3권
1.3

1. Tree
2. Housework
3. Riding a Bike
4. Spider
5. Hobbies
6. Winter

7. Vegetables
8. Sea
9. My Town
10. School Tools
11. Farm Animals
12. Five Senses